MY LIFE WITH THE INDIANS

THE STORY OF MARY JEMISON

WRITTEN BY ROBIN MOORE   ILLUSTRATED BY VICTOR AMBRUS

FRANKLIN WATTS

NEW YORK • LONDON • SYDNEY

FOREWORD

During her seventy-six years among the Seneca Indian people, Mary Jemison survived two wars, outlived two husbands and witnessed some of the most dramatic and tragic events of early American history. She raised eight children, thirty-nine grandchildren and fourteen great-grandchildren in the face of many hardships.

Captured by a Shawnee war party when she was fifteen, Mary's life was spared by two young Seneca women who adopted her as their sister. Although she could have returned to her former life, Mary chose to remain among the Seneca until her death at the age of ninety.

When Mary was asked to tell her story to the writer James Everett Seaver in the winter of 1823, it took the eighty-year-old woman three days, stopping only for meals and sleep, to tell the story of her life. When she finished, Mary Jemison had delivered one of the most remarkable accounts of Indian captivity in our possession.

In her narrative, Mary Jemison was very careful to point out what she felt were admirable aspects of native life and to explain how contacts with the white race had weakened the once-powerful tribe and lead to the collapse of the Great Confederacy of the Iroquois.

A Narrative of the Life of Mrs Mary Jemison was first published in 1824. It was a great success and outsold many novels for the rest of the decade.

But perhaps the best way to hear Mary's story would be to travel back in the imagination to the winter of 1823 and take the snow-covered footpath along the Genesee River to Mary Jemison's cabin on Gardow Flats. Seaver noted that Mary loved visitors and was always known to make welcome the weary traveller.

So let's journey back across the years and listen to Mary's story, as she might have told it herself, if we had stopped by her cabin on a snowy evening in December 1823 . . .

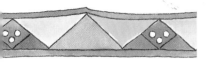 

MY LIFE WITH THE INDIANS

Outside, the wind howls through the frozen trees. Overhead, the cold stars dance in the night sky. Even the great Genesee River is frozen, hard as iron. The snow is knee-deep here on Gardow Flats. Up ahead, a wisp of smoke curls from the chimney of Mary Jemison's cabin.

Inside, a warm fire is burning. The room is filled with lantern light, laughter and the smells of good food: smoked venison and peppery rabbit stew, hot acorn bread and roasted pumpkin seeds, golden maizecakes and baked apples smothered in melted butter and wild honey.

There is always a warm place on a bench by a crackling fire where you can take a seat. And when you are fed and warmed, drowsy with heat and comfort, you hear the sound of the old woman's voice, rising and falling, like the winter wind outside, telling you her story . . .

When I was a girl, we had a fine farm along Marsh Creek, just outside Gettysburg, Pennsylvania. I wish you could have seen our farm. It was like a little piece of paradise, set off by itself in the wilderness.

My father and older brothers had cleared the land eight years before. We had a large flock of sheep and a herd of cattle. We had a good log barn and a sturdy house. Our fields were full of maize and flax. We were never sick or weary like other folks, we considered ourselves to be wealthy and lucky too.

Then, on a fine spring morning in 1758, when I was fifteen years old, our luck ran out. The war between the French and the British was pushing across the frontier, heading in our direction. The French had set the Indian tribes against us, vowing to kill us and burn us out.

And although we had never heard the war cry or seen the smoke from a dwelling lit by an Indian hand, we knew that the raiding parties from the north would someday reach our neck of the woods. My father was sitting in the sunlight on the doorstep that day, shaving an axe handle.

It was early morning and we had not yet had our breakfast. Mother was cooking by the hearthfire and I was beside her, tending my tiny sisters.

Suddenly, we heard a gunshot. I swung open the door and saw a war party of four Frenchmen and six Indians wrestling my father to the ground.

I cried out to him. But before I could do anything else, the warriors were all around me, pushing their way through the door and dragging us outside, hurrying us across the fields and up into the woods.

THE JOURNEY

We had to walk very fast that day, without a drop of water nor a mouthful of food. When the little children began to cry, the Indians drove them along by whipping their legs with a willow switch. Father was forced along by two Frenchmen with bayonets attached to their muskets.

My mother was very brave. She came and walked beside us, telling us not to be afraid and not to cry, she said that we were Jemisons and that we could walk as far as any savage. I knew from the position of the sun that we were heading west, away from towns and farms, deeper into the wilderness. That night we slept on the bare ground in the cold woods, without a fire to warm us or a scrap of blanket to cover our shivering bodies.

The second day was worse than the first. We walked all day, driven along like cattle.

I was wearing ill-fitting shoes which rubbed me painfully with each step. By the time we made camp that night, at the edge of a dismal swamp, my feet were bleeding badly.

It was dark and frosty-cold, with a full moon rising up over the hilltops.

As I sank to the ground, one of the warriors noticed my bloody feet and knelt before me, removing my shoes and stockings and placing a well-made pair of deerskin moccasins on my feet.

When my mother saw this, she began to cry.

Mother knelt beside me and took me into her arms. The tears on her face looked like silver droplets in the moonlight. Then, close to my ear, in whispered words, she said:

"Mary, I can't believe this is happening to us, dear. I can't believe I must say goodbye to you."

"I don't want you to be sad, Mary. But I must tell you the truth: I think the Indians mean to kill us here.

"But because of the moccasins they've placed on your feet, I think they will spare your life and take you back amongst them as a captive.

"Remember your prayers and say them every day. Remember who you are.

"Whatever happens, Mary, I want you to remember that I've always loved you and that –"
But before she could finish, the warrior who had given me the moccasins grasped me by the hand and pulled me from my mother's embrace.

She cried out and reached for me. But there was nothing she could do. My small fingers trailed off the end of hers like the last leaves falling from a tree in winter.

The warrior led me away into the dark wood where he made a bed for me in the leaves.

I knew then that I would never see my natural-born family again.

After four hard days of walking, my captors brought me to Fort Du Quenese, which was occupied by the French and their Indian allies. I was given into the care of two pleasant-looking young Indian women, just a few years older than me.

I later learned that they were from the Seneca nation, one of the six nations of the Great Iroquois Confederacy, and that the men who had taken me were Shawnee, a tribe who lived further down the Ohio River, south of the fort. In those days, the Seneca and the other Iroquois nations held domain over all the neighbouring tribes and travelled freely up and down the river, living and hunting as they desired.

Fort Du Quenese

Iroquois mocassins, highly decorated with glass beads and porcupine quillwork.

My new guardians loaded me into a small canoe made from a hollowed-out log. We set off downriver, following the Shawnee men, who were in larger canoes ahead.

The river was wide and shallow, snaking down through the hills and past rocky cliffs, taking me further away from the land I knew. As we angled out into the current and were swept downstream, I noticed something that made my blood turn to ice in my veins. Dangling from a wooden pole, which jutted out from the bow of the warriors' canoe, were the scalps of my mother, my father, my older brothers and my little sisters.

A wave of fear and disgust rippled through me. For a moment, I wished that I had been killed along with the rest of my family. Why had I been kept alive? Where were these people taking me and what would they do with me once we got there? I wondered if they had only preserved me so that I could be tortured and killed in some savage sacrifice somewhere downstream.

When we arrived at their village later that day, I was prepared for the worst.

SCALPS

Scalps were taken as trophies of war and as a way of collecting the bounties that warring European armies offered Indians in return for killing their enemies.

11

Once we had landed at their camp, the two young women motioned to me to wade into the shallow water with them. They drew their knives and cut away my filthy, tattered dress and threw it into the river. I watched as it sank and was carried away by the current.

They scrubbed my skin clean with handfuls of sand and washed my hair with a sweet-smelling soap. Then they led me up onto the riverbank and produced a bundle containing a beautiful dress made from blue cloth, a set of beaded leggings, and a new pair of elk-hide moccasins. Even though these were not the kind of clothes I was used to, they felt clean and warm and dry against my skin.

As one of the women held my head still, the other pricked a hole in my ear lobes with a splinter of bone and ran a greased string through, hanging a strand of beads on each of my ears. Then they combed and braided my hair.

Before I could wonder any more about these strange preparations, they led me back into a bark house at the centre of the village where many women were gathered around a crackling fire. The air was sharp with the smell of pungent herbs.

The women then began singing, dancing and crying. Soon they were weeping and wailing as if they were mourning the dead. Then, as they regained their composure, they dried their tears and regarded me with joyful, sparkling eyes.

I later learned that this was an adoption ceremony and that I had been taken in by the two young women to replace a brother who had been killed in the war. I was given the name 'Dickewamis', which means 'pretty girl'.

From that day forward, my protectors considered me to be their sister, just as if we had been born of the same mother.

That was when my life as a Seneca woman really began.

Although I missed my family terribly and longed to be back, among my own kind, I spent a pleasant summer there on the Ohio.

My new-found sisters were always gentle and tender to me and took time to teach me their language, culture and customs. Strange as it might seem, I soon came to love them, just as I had my own family, back on the farm.

As winter approached, we brought in an excellent crop of maize and headed down the Ohio River to a place called Scioto, where the men enjoyed good hunting throughout the long winter.

In the spring, we returned to our old camp and planted the fields we had tilled the year before.

In those early days, I never planned to adopt completely the ways of my captors. I always expected that I would return to my former life.

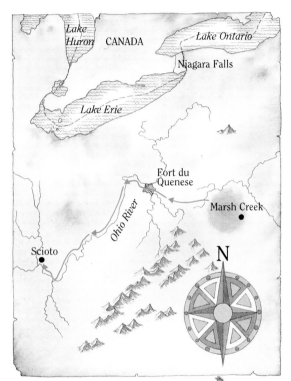

In a secret place in my mind, I said my prayers each day, as a way of keeping the memory of my language and my heritage alive.

But time, the healer of all wounds, worked its way upon me. As the seasons rolled by, my thoughts of escape faded away and I became quite contented with our life along the river.

A NEW BEGINNING

In the third year of my captivity, my sisters announced that they had arranged for me to marry a warrior named Shenijee of the Delaware nation.

At first, the thought of marrying an Indian repelled me. But I obeyed my sisters' wishes and soon learned that the man they had chosen for me was good-natured, generous and tender. As time went on, I came to love him and found him to be an agreeable husband and a pleasant companion.

I later gave birth to my first child, a girl. But, to my great sadness, she died almost immediately. A year later I delivered a healthy son whom I named Thomas Jemison, in memory of my father.

But on the heels of this happy event, Shenijee died of an illness, leaving me a widow.

My sisters came to my aid again and found me a new husband, an excellent Seneca man whom I would be married to for over fifty years. His name was Hiokatoo. With him I had two sons and four daughters. I named them John and Jesse, Nancy, Betsy, Jane and Polly, in remembrance of the family I had lost.

14

After the British defeated the French in 1763, we lived in happiness and peace for fifteen years. During this time Hiokatoo and I moved our family up to the northern Seneca country, up along the Genesee River, just south of Niagara.

There, along the curve of the river, in the Great Genesee Valley, we settled in Little Beard's Town, the largest and finest of the Seneca villages.

This was no cluster of huts in the wood. This was a real town, with over a hundred well-made log houses, laid out neatly along the main road. Each house was surrounded by flowers and gardens and fruit trees. Our cherry and apple orchards were heavy with fruit.

Out beyond the houses were fertile fields of maize, beans and squash. Beyond the fields lay lush grasslands where we grazed our cattle.

And beyond that, the green glades of the forest where we went to collect firewood and hickory nuts and maple syrup.

A person could not help but be happy, living in that fair land. Our wants were few and easily satisfied. I was surrounded by friends and family.

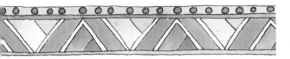 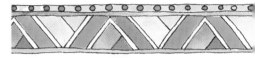

During those years, I was given several opportunities to return to my own people. But, after careful consideration, I decided to remain with my Indian friends.

To anyone who has never lived among the Seneca, this may seem strange. But I felt that I was no longer a captive. I had become a Seneca woman, just as much as if I had been born Seneca.

At Little Beard's Town, I met for the first time other people who were white and had been absorbed into the bosom of Seneca life. These were men and women who had been born French, British or Dutch but who considered themselves, and their children, to be Seneca.

After the war with the French was over, some of the captives were ransomed back. But they went only with the greatest reluctance. A good number of them tried to resume their old lives but soon became disgusted and returned to us, becoming Indians for the rest of their lives.

In the years that I have been among the Indians, I have seen many Europeans become Indians but I have not known a single Indian who has willingly chosen to live in the white world. This may sound curious, but it is true.

Cornplanter was a Seneca chief whose father was a white man.

16

I cannot say why others chose to live as Indians, but I can tell you my reasons.

First and foremost was my concern for my children. They were well loved and well cared for among the Seneca. I knew that if I took them back into white society, they would be despised and hated.

I also knew that my life back among the British would not be so easy or so agreeable.

Seneca women enjoy much more freedom and control over their own lives than their sisters in the white world. Women hold an important and honoured place. It is the women who raise the children and grow the maize. It is the women who can remove chiefs who are not fulfilling their duties. It is the women who are sought for advice and counsel when the Great Iroquois Confederacy meets. If a woman is killed, the blood money that must be paid is twice what it would be if the victim had been a man.

It is important that you understand that the Indians are not savages, as my mother described them. They are a moral and upstanding people, with all the feelings and emotions of their white brethren.

It is true, they can be cruel and brutal in times of war. But many captives were not killed. They were adopted and absorbed into the lifestream of the nation. In this way, the Indians were able to replace members they had lost through war and disease. And once you are adopted into the tribe, nothing is denied you.

In times of peace, no one can live more happily or more harmoniously than the Indians. Their life is their religion and they find their God in forests and meadows, in animals and plants, and in the wind and weather.

17

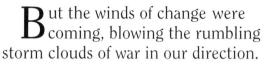

WINDS OF CHANGE

But the winds of change were coming, blowing the rumbling storm clouds of war in our direction.

Just as the French and the British had fought over the land years before, the British King and the American colonies were now preparing to fight over the same land again.

Representatives from the colonies called a great council with the six nations of the Iroquois Confederacy and asked us to make a treaty promising that we would be neutral in the coming war.

Soldiers of the American Revolution.

Our chiefs agreed, for that was the will of the people.

Then, a year later, the British Commissioners came to us and requested our help in subduing the American rebels. Our chiefs said they would not violate the treaty they had made with the people of the colonies.

But the British entreated our warriors with rum, and plied them with arguments and with gifts.

In the end, our men agreed. The British assured our men that the rebels were weak and small in number and could be easily defeated. To prove their point, they invited our warriors to the battle over Fort Stanwix, not to fight, but simply to sit and smoke and look on

as the British army whipped the American rebels.

But they did not simply sit and look on. Instead, they were obliged to fight for their lives. There was a great deal of crying in our town after that battle. This was the beginning of a time that was very bad for us.

Each warrior returned home with a suit of clothes, a brass kettle, a gun and tomahawk, a quantity of powder and lead, a piece of gold and the promise of a bounty on every scalp he could bring in.

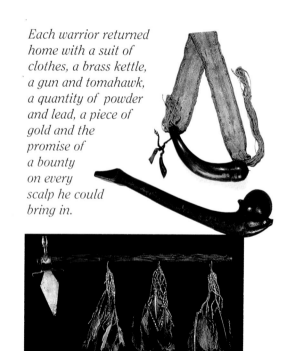

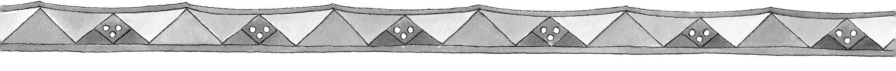

For four or five years, the war dragged on. But the real fighting was going on a hundred miles south and east of us. Then, in the autumn of 1779, our scouts received word that a 5,000-man rebel army, led by General John Sullivan, was sweeping through the Iroquois land, burning all the towns and villages.

Hiokatoo immediately slung his quiver of war arrows onto his back and stuck his war club into his belt. He took the nuggets of charcoal from the fire and began to blacken his face.

On the morning when Sullivan's army came into our valley, swift Seneca runners came through the town, shouting for the women and children to take to the hills, shouting that the men should prepare to fight.

Knowing that I might never see my husband again, I gathered a few blankets and provisions and set off for the woods.

It took three days for the army to reduce Little Beard's Town to a smoking rubble. There was no way they could prevent such a large force from sweeping over us. So we did the only thing we could do: we abandoned our town and watched from the hills as it was burned and ravaged.

After the army moved on, we returned to the ashes of our town and found that the soldiers had ruined everything they could lay their hands on. They had torn up our gardens, chopped down our trees and killed our cattle. Half our maize had been piled inside our houses, then the buildings had been set alight. The other half, they threw into the river. Search as we might, we couldn't find a single handful of food.

The winter was moving in quickly. And my children were hungry and cold.

Gardow Flats

Some of our people went north to winter with the British at Fort Niagara. Some went west and lived on the charity of our neighbouring tribes. Others just scattered and died in the cold forest.

I was going to go north, hoping to meet Hiokatoo at the fort, when I remembered an abandoned log cabin I had once seen at a place called Gardow Flats, along the Genesee River, a few miles south of the town. I thought that I might survive the winter there.

But the cabin was not abandoned. Instead, I found the cabin occupied by two former slaves who had escaped from their masters and taken up residence there on the Flats.

When they saw my frozen and weary children, they offered to share their shelter with us.

Later that night, they explained that they had planted a large field of maize along the river and needed help in harvesting their crop. I readily agreed and we struck a bargain: in return for husking their corn, I could have a portion of the harvest. When the work was done, I had earned twenty-five bushels of shelled maize, enough to feed my children until spring.

The weather during our first winter at Gardow was severe. The snow was five feet deep and the cold was like nothing I had experienced before or since. But, somehow, my children and I struggled through. In fact, I planted and hoed maize there for three years, working with the two men. Then they decided to move on and left me and my children as the sole occupants of the Flats. To my great joy, Hiokatoo returned to us and we were once again a family.

Mary Jemison's original cabin which stood on Gardow Flats.

We stayed on at Gardow Flats. The land was extremely fertile but needed more labour than my children and I could supply. So I began leasing portions of the Flats to white settlers who lived and worked on the land as tenants. This was a good arrangement. My land was well cared for and my children grew like tall maize. When the war ended in 1783, my family was firmly established on the Flats. At the Council of Big Tree in 1797, the Seneca formally granted me a deed for my land. It has ever since been known as the Gardow Tract.

The Indians were of the opinion that the land had been cleared by some ancient race of people who had lived on and tilled the land long before the Seneca had come to this part of the country. I was never able to solve this mystery, I know only that our fields had been planted and hoed for many years. Gardow was good to me in those years. Even as I became older, my health remained excellent and my mind was clear. My children grew up, married and lived nearby, making me a grandmother. But life's sweetest moments are often crowned with tragedy . . .

As my sons grew to manhood, all three learned to drink liquor and often became quarrelsome. My boys were not the only ones who fell under the spell of drink. Many unscrupulous white traders supplied the Indians with alcohol, knowing that they had no resistance to the unfamiliar drink, knowing that, like the diseases which came among the Seneca, drinking would rob the warriors of their strength and pride. After the war, many of our Indian men, and some of the women as well, would gather for rowdy drinking parties. When their tempers became inflamed with the strange drink, they would often become spiteful with one another. Fights would break out and many an Indian awoke from his binge the next morning to find that he had killed a trusted friend or relative.

My boys, too, were unused to the alcohol supplied by white traders and would drink and fight with each other.

Then, on a terrible day in July 1811, my oldest son Thomas and his younger brother John got into a drunken argument while they were visiting my house. In a fit of fury, John snatched up one of my wood axes and struck Thomas a sharp blow on the side of the head. Thomas fell and bled to death, right there on the doorstep of my house. He was then fifty-two years old, the father of many children. John was forty-eight.

Because he had acted in self-defence, the chiefs acquitted John of his brother's murder.

It wasn't long before trouble erupted again, this time between John and my youngest son, Jesse. During a drunken argument, with his hands already stained with the blood of his older brother, John killed Jesse, stabbing him repeatedly with a hunting knife.

John's tormented life ended two years later, when he was killed by two Indians he had been drinking with in the woods.

I had buried three sons, snatched from me by the hand of violence, at a time when I least expected it. To have a child die is a mother's greatest fear. But to have them kill one another – that is too much. It strained my heart to breaking.

As a final blow, my good husband Hiokatoo died, at the advanced age of one hundred and three. Once again, I was a widow on this Earth, but this time with grandchildren to feed. Even though my heart was broken into pieces, my body kept going. The bounty of my land provided for me and my grandchildren. Somehow, we survived.

25

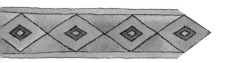 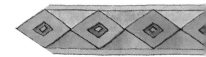

A PRAYER FOR THE FUTURE

My story is almost over. There is not much else I can tell you. I know that in many ways I have been a very lucky woman. I could have been killed by the Shawnee when I was fifteen. But my life was spared by that small gift of moccasins so long ago. I have always been grateful for that.

When I began my new life, as a Seneca woman, I was able to see the land when it was green and growing, when the people were happy and whole, before they became weakened by disease and drink, before the talons of war tore the Great Iroquois Confederacy apart . . .

I still say the prayers my mother taught me. I have continued to pray to my childhood God. But sometimes, my heart, which has suffered so many hardships and disappointments, opens.

And a greater prayer comes forth, a prayer bigger than the one my mother taught me back on Marsh Creek.

I pray that our children's children's children will look back on these years of war and bloodshed and that they will shake their heads at our foolishness and ignorance.

I pray that some day our children, both Indian and white, will clasp hands in friendship and set about the hard work of healing the wounds we have dealt one another.

Then perhaps the land will once again ring with the happy voices of our children.

Perhaps then the council fires will be relit and the people will gather and sit beside one another, letting their prayers rise up and touch the heavens. Perhaps then the story I have told will really mean something.

In the autumn of 1832, Mary Jemison died quietly in her cabin on the Genesee, surrounded by her family. She was ninety years old.

Today, the Seneca still live in the land they have inhabited since ancient times. And, just as Mary Jemison had hoped, the council fires have been relit. The Great Confederacy of the Iroquois has re-formed and is now struggling with its own questions: asking, how can the Iroquois live alongside the white world without being imprisoned by it?

The answer is still in the wind.

But, just as Grandmother Jemison predicted, one by one, Indian and white people are clasping their hands in friendship and beginning the slow, difficult work of building bridges between two very different cultures.

This book is one of many small steps in that direction.

A statue of Mary Jemison was placed in Letchworth State Park, New York State on 19 September 1910.

Mary Jemison witnessed one of the most dramatic and heartbreaking chapters in American history. In the space of a single lifetime, she saw the north-eastern region of North America wrested from the control of the ancient Indian nations and settled by European soldiers, farmers and entrepreneurs.

The story of this conquest is long and complicated.

THE PEOPLE

Mary was a member of the Scottish-Irish group of immigrants who went to the American colonies hoping to obtain land and establish prosperous farms. Unlike the English, the Scottish-Irish immigrants shunned civilization and were the first to head for the wild lands of the frontier, carving their farms out of the great wilderness. The list of Scottish-Irish women who were captured by Indians is long. Many of these women were adopted and became fully-fledged members of the Indian nations.

Mary's story involves three tribes of native Indian people: the Shawnee who took her captive; the Delaware from whom her first husband came and with whom she lived on the Ohio; and the Seneca, who adopted her. It is important to understand that native people did not see themselves as 'Indians'. They saw themselves as members of their respective tribes. It was not until relatively late in their history that they were able to present a united front against what they saw as an invasion by European forces.

THE SHAWNEE

The Shawnee were a war-like, fragmented people who were never united as a single society. They had long-standing conflicts with other Indian nations and were driven from the Ohio Valley by the Iroquois long before Europeans arrived. By the time settlement began, the Shawnee were considered part of the Iroquois Confederacy. They negotiated with the British and the French, playing one off against the other in an attempt to win their own independence.

THE SENECA

The Seneca were one of the six Indian nations who belonged to the Iroquois Confederacy, formed in the early 1600s. Although they were not large in number, these nations occupied a strategic position in what is now New York State and developed a structure that allowed them to extend their influence from Canada to the Carolinas, from the Atlantic Ocean to the Mississippi River. Both France and Britain understood that their contest for control of the region would depend upon which country could form an alliance with the Iroquois and use it to defeat the other.

THE DELAWARE

The Delaware were an ancient people who had inhabited the region of what is now Pennsylvania and New Jersey for at least 3,000 years. Their first European contact was probably with the Italian explorer Giovanni da Verazano in 1524. From that time forward, they were intimately involved in the European fur trade, land acquisitions and diplomatic ventures. By the mid-1600s, they had fallen under the control of the Iroquois. By 1768, the European invasion had pushed the last of the Delaware from their homelands into the Ohio Valley region. By that time, 24,000 Delaware who had once lived in the north-east had been reduced to a mere 3,000 by the ravages of warfare and disease.

George Washington, during the French and Indian War, in the uniform of Colonel, serving the Biritsh cause.

THE WARS

The conquest of the north-east of North America was played out in a series of small wars. The two major conflicts were the French and Indian War and the Revolutionary War. Both occurred within Mary Jemison's lifetime.

THE FRENCH AND INDIAN WAR (1754–1763)

This was a conflict between France and Britain for control of North America. While the British were building a substantial presence on the Atlantic coastline, they were outraged to discover that the French had built a series of forts in the interior. The Governor of Virginia sent a 21-year-old militia officer with a small force to Fort Lebouf to deliver an ultimatum to the French: pull out of North America or prepare for a full-scale war on American soil. The French refused. The war had begun in earnest. The name of the young officer was George Washington.

While the Iroquois tried to remain neutral, they were eventually drawn into the war, fighting on the side of the French. British settlers on the frontier were terrorized by the French and their Indian allies. Attacks like that on the Jemison's farm were widespread, making the wilderness an exceedingly dangerous place. The French were defeated in 1763, giving up their claims to Canada and all lands east of the Mississippi River.

THE REVOLUTIONARY WAR (1775–1783)

This pitted the army of the fledgling American state against the might of the British. Again, the Iroquois were caught in a power struggle between two groups of Europeans. At first, they tried to remain neutral. But, finally, they were drawn into the war. The six nations could not decide on the right course of action. So, in 1777, the council fire of the Great Confederacy was covered and each nation went its own way. General George Washington sent an army under General John Sullivan to burn the Iroquois towns and villages in the summer of 1779. He swept through the region like a firestorm, destroying everything in his path. The Iroquois never recovered from their losses.

When Britain was defeated and a peace treaty was signed in 1783, no provisions were made for the Indian allies. The once-powerful Iroquois became refugees in the land they had regarded as their own.

The political structure of the Iroquois Confederacy, along with its innovative form of representative government, was praised in the writings of Thomas Jefferson and Benjamin Franklin. Some historians believe that the Confederacy may have been used as a model for creating the Constitution of the United States and the government that is now entrusted with former Indian land.

INDEX

PICTURE CREDITS

Brigitte Saal, Museum für Völkerunde, Hamburg: p9
British Museum: pp 11, 18 centre right and bottom right
Norman and Sylvia Bancroft-Hunt (British Museum): p18 top right
Peter Newark's American Pictures: pp 16, 18 left, 20
Clark Rice, The Little Studio, NY: pp 23, 27, 29

Text © Robin Moore
Illustrations © Victor Ambrus

Franklin Watts Australia, 14 Mars Road,
Lane Cove, NSW

UK ISBN: 0 7496 2363 2
10 9 8 7 6 5 4 3 2 1

Dewey Decimal Classification 970.004

Editor: Kyla Barber
Designer: Kate Buxton
Art Director: Robert Walster
Map artwork: Sallie Reason
Border artwork: Kate Buxton

A CIP catalogue record for this book is
available from the British Library

Printed in Singapore

DEDICATION

This Book is dedicated to the memory of my grandmothers,
Romaine McCord Baer and Adeline Burris Moore:
rural Pennsylvania women who, like Mary Jemison, asked their
own questions and made their own choices.

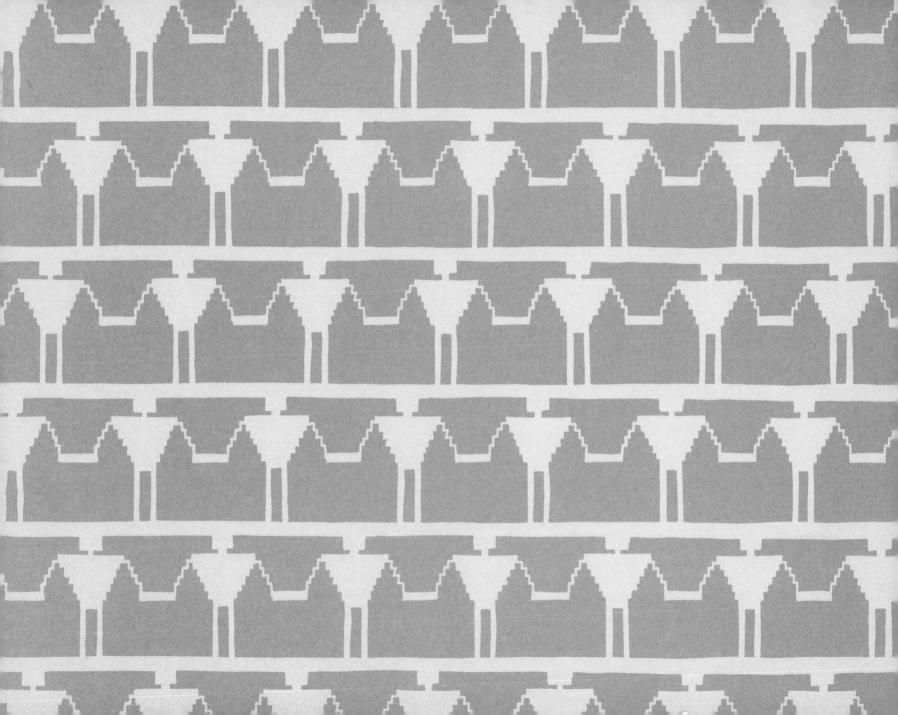